I0606099

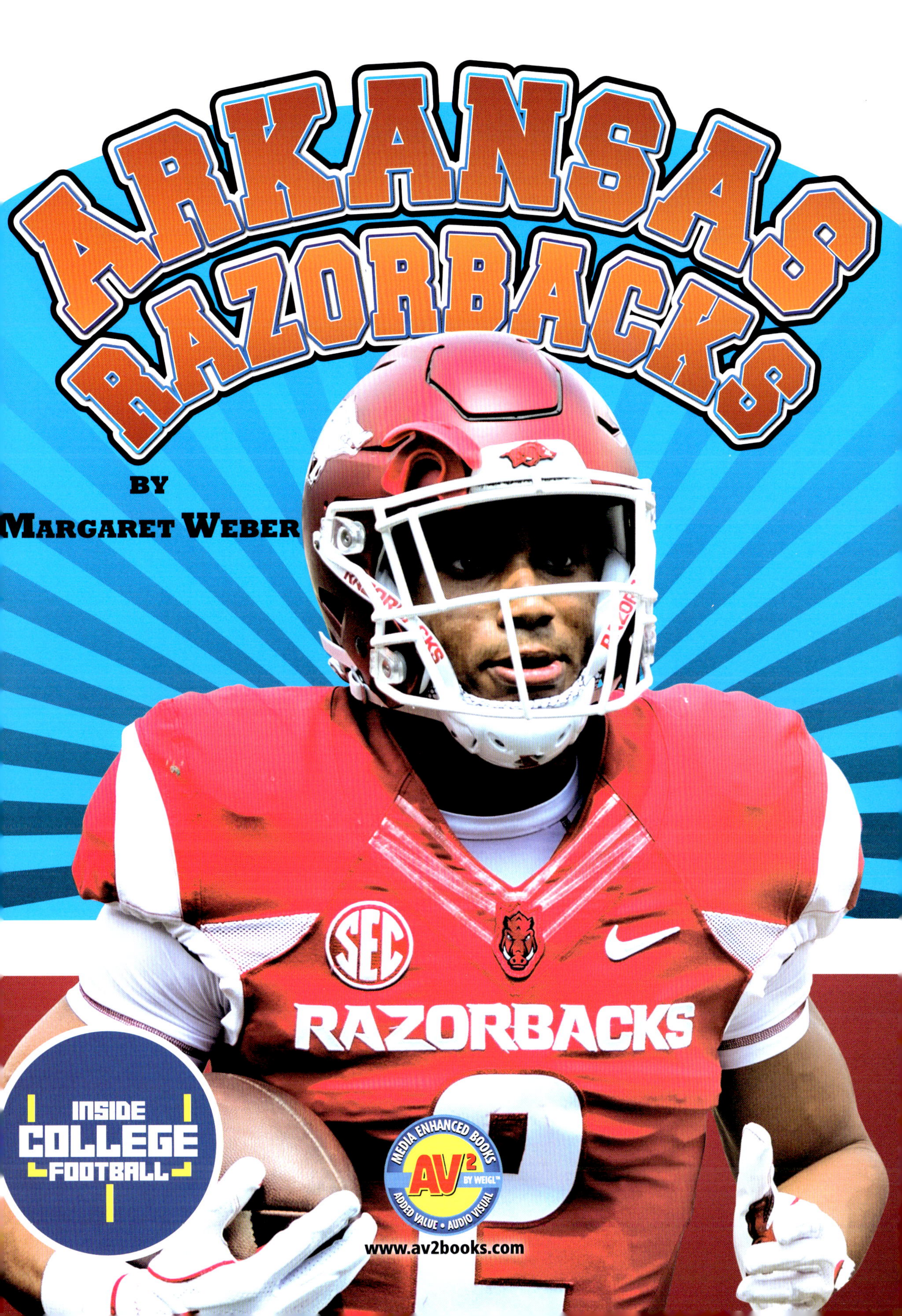
ARKANSAS
RAZORBACKS
BY
MARGARET WEBER
SEC
RAZORBACKS
INSIDE
COLLEGE
FOOTBALL
MEDIA ENHANCED BOOKS
AV2
BY WEIGL
ADDED VALUE • AUDIO VISUAL
www.av2books.com

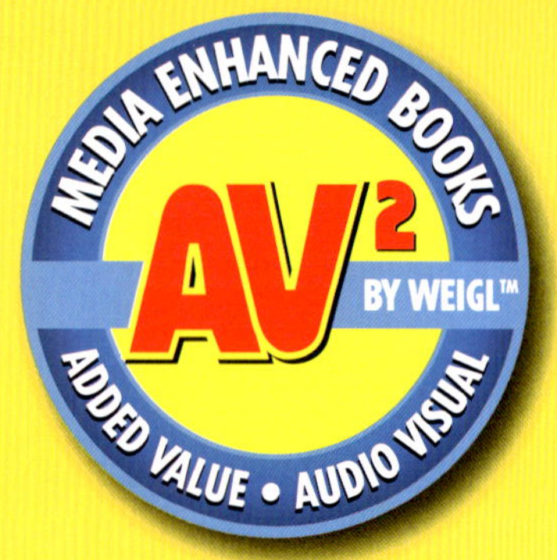

Go to www.av2books.com, and enter this book's unique code.

BOOK CODE

AVH74587

AV² by Weigl brings you media enhanced books that support active learning.

AV² provides enriched content that supplements and complements this book. Weigl's AV² books strive to create inspired learning and engage young minds in a total learning experience.

Your AV² Media Enhanced books come alive with...

Audio
Listen to sections of the book read aloud.

Key Words
Study vocabulary, and complete a matching word activity.

Video
Watch informative video clips.

Quizzes
Test your knowledge.

Embedded Weblinks
Gain additional information for research.

Slideshow
View images and captions, and prepare a presentation.

Try This!
Complete activities and hands-on experiments.

... and much, much more!

Published by AV² by Weigl
350 5th Avenue, 59th Floor
New York, NY 10118
Website: www.av2books.com

Library of Congress Control Number: 2018968226

ISBN 978-1-7911-0135-0 (hardcover)
ISBN 978-1-7911-0136-7 (multi-user eBook)
ISBN 978-1-7911-0137-4 (single-user eBook)

Printed in Guangzhou, China
1 2 3 4 5 6 7 8 9 0 23 22 21 20 19

042019
102318

Project Coordinator: Jared Siemens   Designer: Terry Paulhus

The publisher acknowledges Alamy, Getty Images, and Wikimedia Commons as its primary image suppliers for this title.

Arkansas Razorbacks

CONTENTS

Introduction

The University of Arkansas is in Fayetteville, Arkansas. It is represented by the Razorbacks football team in the National Collegiate Athletic Association (NCAA). The Razorbacks are also known by the nickname "Hogs." The team is currently ranked 21st for all-time wins in college football.

Many fans know the Razorbacks for their **rivalries**. One of their earlier rivalries was with the University of Texas Longhorns, which began in 1894. This rivalry died down in 1991, when the teams no longer shared a conference. Today, many fans are drawn to the Razorbacks' rivalry with the Louisiana State University (LSU) Tigers. These two teams compete for a 175-pound (79 kilograms), 4-foot (1.21 meters) gold trophy in the shape of Arkansas and Louisiana. The outline of the two states forms the shape of a boot, and the trophy is known as the Golden Boot.

Wide receiver Jordan Jones made 38 receptions for 592 yards and scored two touchdowns in 2017 and 2018, his first two seasons on the field for the Razorbacks.

The University of Arkansas is also known for attracting strong players. There have been 49 Arkansas players awarded **All-American** honors. Many Razorbacks players have also gone on to careers in the National Football League (NFL).

Offensive lineman Colton Jackson was one of the 2017 season's most effective players for the Razorbacks. Jackson started 10 out of 12 games and allowed only one quarterback sack for the season.

ARKANSAS

Stadium Donald W. Reynolds Razorback Stadium

Division Southeastern Conference (SEC) Western

Head Coach Chad Morris

Location Fayetteville, Arkansas

National Championships 1

Nicknames Razorbacks, Hogs

9
Players in the College Football Hall of Fame

13
Conference Championships

23
First-Round NFL Draft Picks

42
Bowl Games Played

History

In 1964, the year the Razorbacks won a **National Championship**, they were the only team to go undefeated in college football.

Under Coach Ken Hatfield, who was a defensive back on Arkansas's 1964 National Championship team, the Razorbacks won back-to-back Southwest Conference titles in 1988 and 1989.

College football came to the University of Arkansas in 1894. The first team was coached by John Futrall. Futrall was also a Latin professor at the university. The early teams were known as the Cardinals. In 1910, the team's name changed to the Razorbacks. A razorback is a type of wild pig. Fans have been cheering for the Hogs ever since. In 1915, the team joined the Southwest Conference, along with six other teams from Texas and Oklahoma.

The Razorbacks made a national name for themselves in the 1960s and 1970s. During these decades, the team was often competing for national titles. In 1964, the Razorbacks were named national champions. In 1969, the Razorbacks played a game against the Texas Longhorns that is known as "The Big Shootout." The Longhorns beat the Hogs by only one point in a game considered one of the most memorable the two schools have ever played against each other.

The Razorbacks joined the Southeastern Conference (SEC) in 1992. In 2008, Bobby Petrino coached his first season for the Razorbacks. He led the team to an unexpected last-second win over the LSU Tigers the day after Thanksgiving. Moments like this show the Hogs' potential. Today, Chad Morris is coach, and the team looks ahead to more wins and championships.

The first year it was known as the Razorbacks, the Arkansas football team finished the season with a 7–0 record that included 4 shutouts and a combined total of 186 points.

The Stadium

Donald W. Reynolds Razorback Stadium has undergone numerous expansions since it was opened in 1938. The stadium's initial capacity was just less than 14,000 people. It currently seats more than 76,000 fans, with a record attendance of 76,808 set in 2010.

The Razorbacks' home stadium is Donald W. Reynolds Razorback Stadium. The team has played there since 1938. From 1941 to 2001, it was known simply as Razorback Stadium. The stadium underwent major **renovations** between 2000 and 2001. In 2001, the stadium was renamed in honor of the Donald W. Reynolds Foundation, which donated $20 million for renovations and improvements.

Some Razorbacks home games are also played at War Memorial Stadium. War Memorial Stadium is in Little Rock, Arkansas. Since 2014, the team has played one home game per season there. This allows fans from other areas of Arkansas to attend Razorbacks games.

One of the highlights of game days for the Razorbacks is the Razorbacks Marching Band, which is nicknamed the "Best in Sight and Sound." There are more than 350 members in the band. It entertains fans with songs such as the "Arkansas Fight." Spectators at Donald W. Reynolds Razorback stadium watch the action from all sides of the field. The student section is on the southeast side of the stadium. It offers a close view of both the game and the band.

The Best in Sight and Sound is the largest student organization at the University of Arkansas. The band has won multiple awards and has performed at many bowl games, including the Cotton Bowl and the Sugar Bowl.

Where They Play

Welcome to Donald W. Reynolds Razorback Stadium, home of the University of Arkansas Razorbacks. Since 1938, fans have flocked to the stadium to watch the Razorbacks take on rivals on their home turf. The stands are filled with red and white, and the Best in Sight and Sound marches in formation as the team takes the field. The Razorbacks are ready to win.

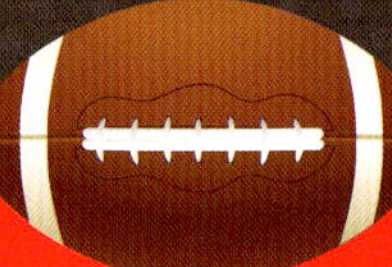

SEC WEST

1 **Auburn University**
Auburn, Alabama

2 **Louisiana State University**
Baton Rouge, Louisiana

3 **Mississippi State University**
Starkville, Mississippi

4 **Texas A&M University**
College Station, Texas

5 **University of Alabama**
Tuscaloosa, Alabama

☆6 **University of Arkansas**
Fayetteville, Arkansas

7 **University of Mississippi**
Oxford, Mississippi

Arena
Donald W. Reynolds Razorback Stadium

Location
Fayetteville, Arkansas

Broke Ground
1937

Completed
1938

Surface
Artificial Turf

Features
- Frank Broyles Field is named for the team's former coach
- A 38-foot (12-meter) high and 167-foot (51-m) wide LED Scoreboard
- Six 20-foot (6-m) tall hog statues guard the exterior of the stadium

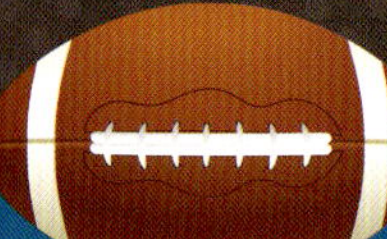

SEC EAST

1 **University of Florida**
Gainesville, Florida

2 **University of Georgia**
Athens, Georgia

3 **University of Kentucky**
Lexington, Kentucky

4 **University of Missouri**
Columbia, Missouri

5 **University of South Carolina**
Columbia, South Carolina

6 **University of Tennessee**
Knoxville, Tennessee

7 **Vanderbilt University**
Nashville, Tennessee

NORTH DAKOTA
SOUTH DAKOTA
MINNESOTA
WISCONSIN
MICHIGAN
NEW YORK
NEW HAMPSHIRE
VERMONT
MAINE
MASSACHUSETTS
RHODE ISLAND
CONNECTICUT
NEW JERSEY
PENNSYLVANIA
DELAWARE
MARYLAND
WASHINGTON, D.C.
NEBRASKA
IOWA
ILLINOIS
INDIANA
OHIO
WEST VIRGINIA
VIRGINIA
KANSAS
MISSOURI
KENTUCKY
NORTH CAROLINA
TENNESSEE
SOUTH CAROLINA
OKLAHOMA
ARKANSAS
MISSISSIPPI
ALABAMA
GEORGIA
TEXAS
LOUISIANA
FLORIDA
Atlantic Ocean
Gulf of Mexico
1
2
3
4
5
6
7
1
2
3
4
5
7
6
N
E
S
W
SCALE
0 miles
500 miles
0 kilometers
500 km
LEGEND
Home Stadium
SEC West
SEC East
United States
Other Countries
Water

The Uniforms

There are no **words** or **numbers** on the Razorbacks helmet, only the Razorbacks logo.

The stripes on Arkansas's uniforms are made to resemble wild hog tusks. The font on the jerseys also includes a point similar to a tusk. The tusk design has been a part of the uniform design in some form since the early 2000s.

The official colors of the University of Arkansas and the Razorbacks are cardinal and white. Cardinal is a specific shade of red. It is slightly darker than a traditional red color. There have been changes to the uniforms throughout the years. Although uniform styles have changed, the colors have not.

For the 2018 season, the Razorbacks **unveiled** a new and updated uniform. The university calls the changes its "Modern Style + Traditional Fire." The helmet is painted a smooth and shiny cardinal red color that helps it stand out on the field. The cardinal jersey has white lettering and white stripes on the shoulder. The word "Razorbacks" is written across the front in capital letters, just above the player number. The pants are white and there is a cardinal stripe on the side of the pants that mirrors the white stripe on the jersey sleeve. All of the player uniforms are made in partnership with **Nike**.

In their 2018 season opener against the Eastern Illinois University Panthers, the Razorbacks wore white helmets for the first time since 2014.

Student Athletes

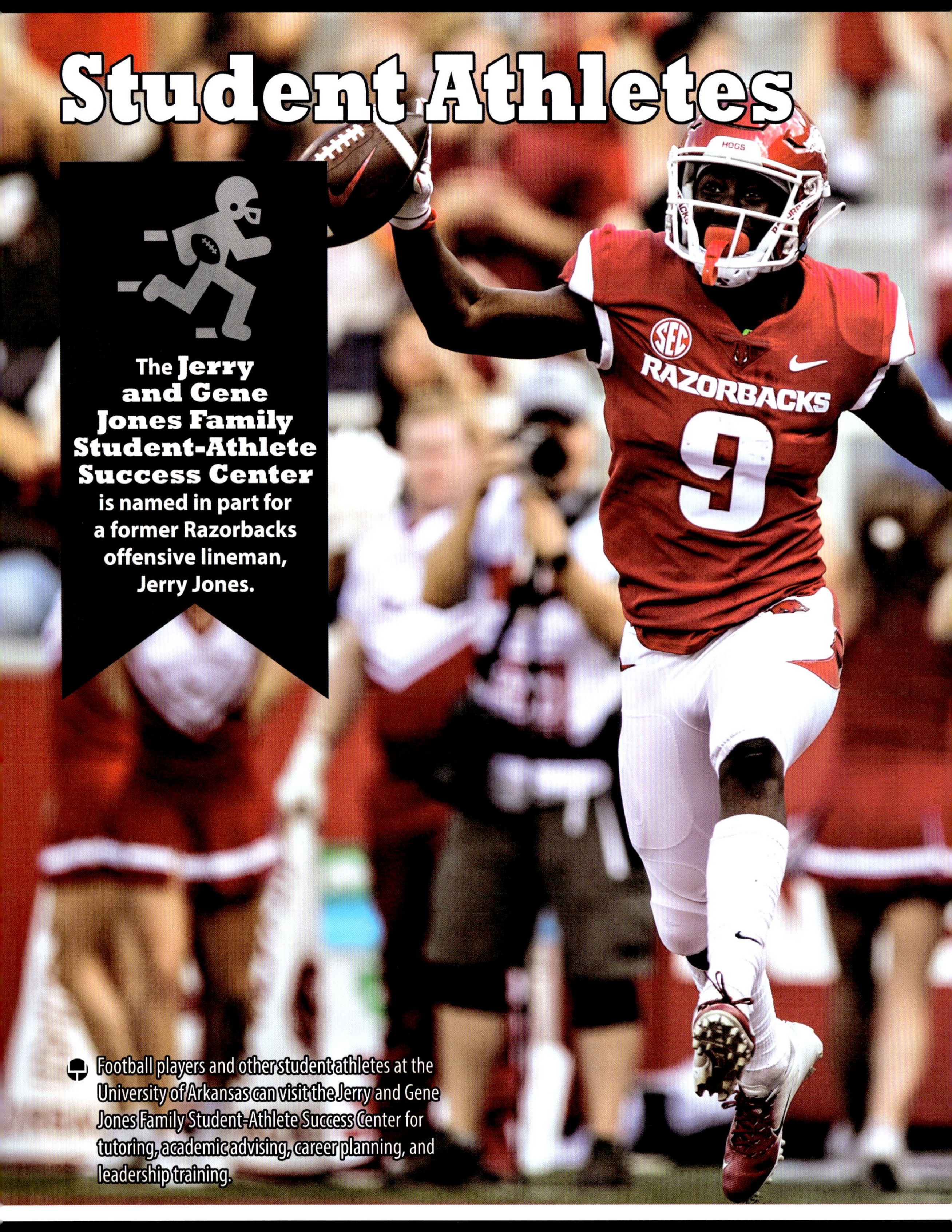

The **Jerry and Gene Jones Family Student-Athlete Success Center** is named in part for a former Razorbacks offensive lineman, Jerry Jones.

Football players and other student athletes at the University of Arkansas can visit the Jerry and Gene Jones Family Student-Athlete Success Center for tutoring, academic advising, career planning, and leadership training.

Being a college student athlete is hard work. Student athletes have to perform well on the football field and in the classroom. University of Arkansas student athletes are required to meet a minimum grade point average and attend all of their classes. They must also have 12 academic credits per term.

Many student athletes are given athletic scholarships, which are financial aid agreements between the athlete and the college or university. Athletes who do not receive an athletic scholarship can also be "walk-on" members of the team. This means they are on the team, but without athletic financial aid. The University of Arkansas typically awards the maximum number of football scholarships allowed, which is 85.

The University of Arkansas is committed to helping its student athletes succeed. Every year, it holds a Student Athlete Recognition Night. During the event, players are honored for their hard work. Graduating seniors also receive a plaque that includes an action photo of themselves and a space for their diploma.

In his freshman season with the Razorbacks, backup quarterback Connor Noland completed 21 passes for 255 yards and a touchdown. Noland was the number-two high school player in the state of Arkansas when he accepted a scholarship to play for the Razorbacks in 2018.

Bowl Games

The **longest** streak of bowl appearances for the Razorbacks is **six in a row**, which they have done **three times**, most recently between **1998** and **2003**.

The Razorbacks went to three consecutive bowl games under the leadership of Head Coach Bret Bielema, including the team's most recent bowl game, the 2016 Belk Bowl. The Virginia Tech Hokies defeated the Razorbacks 35–24 in the Belk Bowl.

After the college football season ends, a rare sports tradition begins. There is no NCAA-sponsored **postseason** for the sport of football. Instead, a variety of games called bowl games are played. There are currently 40 bowl games played between college football teams. These games give teams the chance to play rivals or new teams. It is also a chance to compete for respect and wins even after they have finished with the regular season. The game **matchups** are announced in December.

The Hogs have made 42 appearances in bowl games. Their first bowl game was the 1934 Dixie Classic, which ended in a 7–7 tie against Centenary College. Their overall bowl record is 15–24–3. In the 1947 Cotton Bowl, the Razorbacks faced the LSU Tigers. The temperatures were so cold during the game that players had to compete in **sleet**, ice, and snow. It is remembered today as "The Ice Bowl." The game ended in a 0–0 tie.

Both Arkansas and the Louisiana State University Tigers received Cotton Bowl trophies in 1947, after the game ended in a scoreless tie. The Razorbacks won the original trophy in a coin toss, and a copy was created for LSU later that year.

The Coaches

Chad Morris is one of only five Division I football coaches currently in the NCAA who **did not** play college football.

As offensive coordinator under Head Coach Dabo Swinney at Clemson University, Chad Morris developed an offensive style that Swinney now refers to as "Clemson Offense," a playing style that has won the team two National Championships since Morris left the team.

There have been 33 head coaches in the Razorbacks' history. Football coaches often rely on a team of coaches to help their team achieve wins or make it to the championships. However, head coaches are remembered for everything that happens on the field while they are in charge. For the Razorbacks, there have been a few standouts who have impacted the team.

FRANK BROYLES Frank Broyles is often credited with making the Razorbacks the team it is today. During his 19 years as head coach, from 1958 to 1976, Broyles led the team to 144 wins. He is the winningest coach in Razorbacks history. He also led the team to seven Southwest Conference championships. Broyles retired from coaching in 1976, but remained with the university as athletic director until 2007.

LOU HOLTZ Lou Holtz joined the Razorbacks from North Carolina State University in 1977. In his first season, Holtz led the team to a 10–1 record. During his first six seasons as coach, Holtz helped the team win seven or more games each season. He also took the Hogs to a bowl game in each of his first six seasons. Holtz left Arkansas in 1983 to become head coach at the University of Minnesota.

CHAD MORRIS Chad Morris joined the Razorbacks in 2017. He came to Arkansas from Southern Methodist University, where he improved his record significantly each season he coached. Morris's win record was 2–10 during his first season at Southern Methodist, and 7–6 during his third and most recent season there. Morris also led the Clemson University Tigers' offense to four winning seasons during his time as Clemson's offensive coordinator/quarterbacks coach.

The Mascot

Big Red is the original costumed Razorbacks mascot. He debuted in the 1970s and has been a recognizable part of Arkansas's spirit squad ever since, pumping up fans and dancing on the sidelines.

The University of Arkansas Razorbacks are represented by two mascots. One is a live **Russian boar** named Tusk. The first live boar appeared on the sidelines in the 1960s, but Tusk became the name of the university's official mascot in 1997. There have been five live Tusks, all from the same lineage and raised by the same local family. All of the Tusks have been male, because female boars do not have tusks. Tusk V is the current mascot, and he lives in a large habitat on a farm off-campus.

The other Razorbacks mascot is a costumed boar named "Big Red." He wears a team uniform and runs onto the field with the team before games. Big Red is often joined by a family of costumed boars, including Sue E. Pig, who is dressed as a cheerleader, and Pork Chop, a child-sized razorback. Big Red has been a part of the Arkansas spirit squad since 1973. He is known for his energetic dance moves.

Arkansas fans are famous for "Calling the Hogs." Fans raise their hands over their heads to begin the chant. They call out, "Woooooooo! Pig! Sooie!" As they are calling, they wiggle their fingers, bring their arms down and up, and finish by raising one fist in the air. This is one of the most recognizable chants in college football.

Tusk IV retired after the 2018 season. His son, Tusk V, took over his official mascot duties.

Legends of the Past

For many players, their time with the Razorbacks is the start of a promising football career. These are some of the best-known football players to play for the University of Arkansas.

Trey Flowers

Trey Flowers enrolled at the University of Arkansas and began playing with the Razorbacks in 2011. As a freshman, Flowers appeared in all 13 games for the team. He made 28 tackles in his first season. This included 5.5 tackles for loss during the season. Flowers also started in every game of his sophomore year and missed only one start during his junior year. Flowers finished his time at Arkansas with 190 total tackles. He was drafted by the New England Patriots in 2015, where he remains a vital part of the Patriots' defensive line.

Position: Defensive End
Seasons: 2011–2014 (Arkansas Razorbacks), 2015–Present (New England Patriots)
Born: August 16, 1993, Huntsville, Alabama

Travis Swanson

The first year Travis Swanson played for the Razorbacks, the team led the SEC in passing. As the Hogs' starting center, Swanson was named to the SEC All-Freshman team. He started every game during his sophomore year. In Swanson's junior year, he was named team captain. He also started in every game during that season. The Razorbacks offensive line was ranked third in the conference for sacks allowed, with an average of fewer than two per game. Swanson joined the Miami Dolphins in 2018 after playing four seasons for the Detroit Lions.

Position: Center
Seasons: 2010–2013 (Arkansas Razorbacks), 2014–2017 (Detroit Lions), 2018–Present (Miami Dolphins)
Born: January 30, 1991, Concord, California

Brandon Allen

Brandon Allen's first playing season for the Razorbacks was in 2012. He served as the backup quarterback until 2013, when he became the starting quarterback. That season, Allen had 13 touchdowns. He also passed for 1,552 yards. In his junior year, Allen passed for 2,285 yards. His junior year ended with the 2014 Texas Bowl, where the Razorbacks faced the Texas Longhorns. Allen had two touchdowns during the game and the Hogs won 31–7. Allen was named **Most Valuable Player (MVP)** of the game. Allen currently plays for the Los Angeles Rams.

Position: Quarterback
Seasons: 2012–2015 (Arkansas Razorbacks), 2016 (Jacksonville Jaguars), 2017–Present (Los Angeles Rams)
Born: September 5, 1992, Fayetteville, Arkansas

Hunter Henry

Hunter Henry played for the Razorbacks for three seasons, from 2013 to 2015. He is remembered best by Hogs fans for a play he made in 2015. The Razorbacks were playing against their rivals, the University of Mississippi Rebels. The game had gone into overtime. After catching a pass from the quarterback, Henry made a blind lateral pass to the running back. This led to a touchdown that won the game. Henry was awarded the John Mackey Award that season as well. Henry was part of the Razorbacks team that won two consecutive bowl games for the first time in the school's history. Today, Henry plays for the Los Angeles Chargers.

Position: Tight End
Seasons: 2013–2015 (Arkansas Razorbacks), 2016–Present (Los Angeles Chargers)
Born: December 7, 1994, Little Rock, Arkansas

All-Time Records

7
Single-Game Touchdown Passes
Brandon Allen threw seven touchdowns in a game against the Mississippi State University Bulldogs in November 2015, setting a Razorbacks single-game record.

77
Career Touchdowns
Quarterback Matt Jones scored 53 passing touchdowns and 24 rushing touchdowns from 2001 to 2004. His 77 total touchdowns is a career record for the Razorbacks.

321

Single-Game Rushing Yards

Darren McFadden holds the record for most rushing yards, with 321 in a game against the University of South Carolina Gamecocks in 2007.

61

Career Field Goals

During his career as a Razorback between 2010 and 2013, Zach Hocker made 61 field goals, the all-time record for the team.

485

Single-Season Points

The Razorbacks set a season record in 2007 when they scored a total of 485 points, the highest in Arkansas history.

Timeline

Throughout the team's history, the Arkansas Razorbacks have had many memorable events that have become defining moments for the team and its fans.

1909
The Cardinals go undefeated under Coach Hugo Bezdek.

Coach Bezdek famously says his team plays "like a wild band of razorback hogs," and the team name is officially changed from the Cardinals to the Razorbacks in 1910.

1920s
An important Razorbacks tradition is born when fans begin to cheer for the team with hog calls, calling, "Wooooooo! Pig! Sooie!"

1947
The Razorbacks play Louisiana State University in the Cotton Bowl, and unexpected snowy weather turns the game into "The Ice Bowl."

1964
The 1964 Razorbacks are considered the greatest University of Arkansas team of all time. They are the only team in the country to be undefeated throughout the regular season and postseason.

1900 | 1920 | 1940 | 1960

1976
The Cotton Bowl Classic sees Arkansas return from behind to beat the University of Georgia Bulldogs in Coach Broyles' final game with the Razorbacks.

The Future
The Arkansas Razorbacks are in a period of transition. With a new coach leading the way, the Razorbacks are looking to make their mark in the SEC, as well as on the national stage. The Hogs have a winning history to drive them forward, and their sights are set on defeating their rivals, ranking in college football's top 25, and winning a second National Championship.

2002
The Razorbacks tie a game against Louisiana with only 20 seconds left to play, and David Carlton makes a 35-yard kick to seal the win. The game is known as the "Miracle on Markham."

2007
Coach Broyles is honored when the field at Donald W. Reynolds Razorbacks Stadium is renamed Frank Broyles Field.

1980 — 2000 — 2020

Arkansas moves on to its second conference when it joins the SEC in 1992.

2017
Chad Morris becomes the 33rd head coach of the Razorbacks.

1969
The game known as "The Big Shootout" is played against the Texas Longhorns, with President Richard Nixon in attendance.

2001
On November 3, the Razorbacks make NCAA history when they participate in the first college football game to go into seven overtimes. The Razorbacks defeat the University of Mississippi 58–56.

Write a Biography

Life Story

A person's life story can be the subject of a book. This kind of book is called a biography. Biographies often describe the lives of people who have achieved great success. These people may be alive today, or they may have lived many years ago. Reading a biography can help you learn more about a great person.

Get the Facts

Use this book, and research in the library and on the internet, to find out more about your favorite player. Learn as much about him as you can. What position does he play? What are his statistics in important categories? Has he set any records? Also, be sure to write down key events in the person's life. What was his childhood like? What has he accomplished off the field? Is there anything else that makes this person special or unusual?

Use the Concept Web

A concept web is a useful research tool. Read the questions in the concept web on the following page. Answer the questions in your notebook. Your answers will help you write a biography.

Concept Web

Adulthood

- Where does this individual currently reside?
- Does he have a family?

Your Opinion

- What did you learn from the books you read in your research?
- Would you suggest these books to others?
- Was anything missing from these books?

Childhood

- Where and when was he born?
- Describe his parents, siblings, and friends.
- Did he grow up in unusual circumstances?

Accomplishments off the Field

- What is this person's life's work?
- Has he received awards or recognition for accomplishments?
- How have this person's accomplishments served others?

Write a Biography

Help and Obstacles

- Did this individual have a positive attitude?
- Did he receive help from others?
- Did this person have a mentor?
- Did this person face any hardships?
- If so, how were the hardships overcome?

Accomplishments on the Field

- What records does this person hold?
- What key games and plays have defined his career?
- What are his stats in categories important to his position?

Work and Preparation

- What was this person's education?
- What was his work experience?
- How does this person work?
- What is the process he uses?

Trivia Time

Take this quiz to test your knowledge of the Arkansas Razorbacks. The answers are printed upside down under each question.

1 Where is the University of Arkansas located?

A. Fayetteville, Arkansas

2 The Hogs and the LSU Tigers compete for which trophy?

A. The Golden Boot

3 In what year did the Razorbacks play the Longhorns in "The Big Shootout"?

A. 1969

4 Who is the current coach of the Razorbacks?

A. Chad Morris

5 When did the team's stadium open?

A. 1938

6 What is the nickname of the Razorbacks Marching Band?

A. The "Best in Sight and Sound"

7 What Arkansas game was known as "The Ice Bowl"?

A. The 1947 Cotton Bowl

8 How many head coaches have the Razorbacks had?

A. 33

9 What is the Arkansas fan chant known as?

A. "Calling the Hogs"

10 Who threw a record seven touchdowns in a game against Mississippi State in 2015?

A. Brandon Allen

Key Words

All-American: a player, usually in high school or college, judged to be the best in each position of a sport

matchups: contests between two athletes or sports teams

Most Valuable Player (MVP): the player judged to be most valuable to his team's success

Nike: a brand of athletic clothing that is primarily known for shoes

postseason: a sporting event that takes place after the end of the regular season

renovations: construction that works to improve or expand an older building

rivalries: competitions between different groups or individuals toward the same objective or goal

Russian boar: a wild pig that has tusks that curl up and out of its mouth

sleet: freezing rain and ice pellets

unveiled: to show something in public for the first time

Index

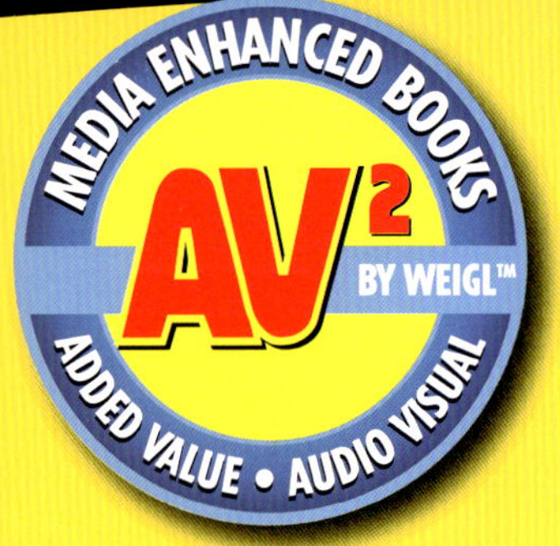

Log on to www.av2books.com

AV² by Weigl brings you media enhanced books that support active learning. Go to www.av2books.com, and enter the special code found on page 2 of this book. You will gain access to enriched and enhanced content that supplements and complements this book. Content includes video, audio, weblinks, quizzes, a slideshow, and activities.

AV² Online Navigation

Audio
Listen to sections of the book read aloud.

Book Pages
AV² pages directly correspond to pages in the book.

Video
Watch informative video clips.

Embedded Weblinks
Gain additional information for research.

Key Words
Study vocabulary, and complete a matching word activity.

Try This!
Complete activities and hands-on experiments.

Quizzes
Test your knowledge.

Slideshow
View images and captions, and prepare a presentation.

AV² was built to bridge the gap between print and digital. We encourage you to tell us what you like and what you want to see in the future.

Sign up to be an AV² Ambassador at www.av2books.com/ambassador.

Due to the dynamic nature of the internet, some of the URLs and activities provided as part of AV² by Weigl may have changed or ceased to exist. AV² by Weigl accepts no responsibility for any such changes. All media enhanced books are regularly monitored to update addresses and sites in a timely manner. Contact AV² by Weigl at 1-866-649-3445 or av2books@weigl.com with any questions, comments, or feedback.